BRITISH RAILWAYS

PAST and PRESENT

No 57

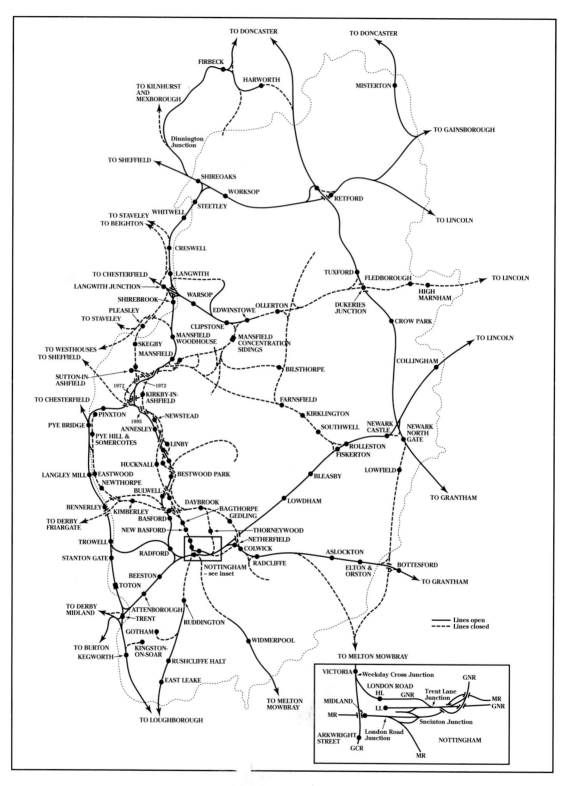

Map of the area covered by this book, owing locations featured or referred to in the text. For clarity some minor a d colliery lines have been omitted.

BRITISH RAILWAYS
PAST and PRESENT

No 57
Nottinghamshire

Paul Shannon

Past & Present Publishing Ltd

First published in 2007

British Library Cataloguing in Publication Data

A catalogue record for this book is available from the British Library.

ISBN 978 1 85895 253 6

Past & Present Publishing Ltd
The Trundle
Ringstead Road
Great Addington
Kettering
Northants NN14 4BW

Tel/Fax: 01536 330588
email: sales@nostalgiacollection.com
Website: www.nostalgiacollection.com

Printed and bound in Great Britain

TUXFORD: Streamlined Class 'A4' 4-6-2 No 60034 *Lord Faringdon* **passes the disused platforms at Tuxford North with the up 'Northumbrian' on 20 August 1960. Local passenger services were never a priority on the busy East Coast Main Line and Tuxford North had closed in 1955. The longest-lived intermediate station between Newark and Retford was Crow Park, which closed in 1958.**

Despite electrification, the train operator GNER maintains a fleet of InterCity 125 units for services running beyond the electrified network, such as Harrogate, Aberdeen and Inverness. An InterCity 125 unit heads south on 23 July 2005. *David Holmes/PDS*

CONTENTS

HUCKNALL BYRON (MR): Stanier Class 4 2-6-4T No 42618 calls at the former Midland Railway station at Hucknall with the 3.11pm train from Nottingham Midland to Worksop on 14 February 1962. The surroundings leave no doubt as to the dominant industry of the area.

Hucknall was chosen as the terminus of Nottingham Express Transit Line One, affording cross-platform interchange with the 'Robin Hood Line', good connections with local bus services and a free car park with more than 400 spaces. A service frequency of between 10 and 12 minutes is maintained for most of the day and the journey time of 28 minutes to central Nottingham would be hard to beat by car. A well-loaded afternoon arrival is pictured on 2 July 2005. *David Holmes/PDS*

INTRODUCTION

A glance at the map on Page 2 shows the contrasting fortunes of Nottinghamshire's railways: a core network of inter-city and secondary passenger routes continues to link the main population centres, now including Mansfield since the successful 'Robin Hood Line' revival, but the one-time proliferation of local lines around Nottingham is a distant memory and the numerous branch lines east of Mansfield have been abandoned together with the coal mines they were built to serve.

Many of the 'past' photographs in this volume date from the 1950s and 1960s, before the infamous Beeching Report had made its full impact. But in reality Beeching was not quite the watershed in Nottinghamshire that it was in many parts of the country. The ridiculous duplication of routes in the Leen Valley north of Nottingham had already been eased, with the GNR line losing its passenger services as early as 1931, while the Mansfield-Southwell line and the Nottingham Suburban Railway via Thorneywood had closed to regular passenger traffic in 1929 and 1931 respectively. More routes had been downgraded or closed in the 1950s, including the former GCR Shirebrook-Tuxford-Lincoln and Kirkby-Mansfield-Clipstone lines.

The relatively few closures of the Beeching period were nonetheless significant. They included the Great Central main line, which had confidently struck through the heart of Nottinghamshire on its way from Manchester and Sheffield to London, and passenger services on the Nottingham-Worksop line, which had connected numerous mining communities such as Kirkby-in-Ashfield, Mansfield and Shirebrook. Other losses during the 1960s were Nottingham to Melton Mowbray, the Southwell branch and the former GNR lines from Gedling across the north side of Nottingham to Pinxton and Derby Friargate.

In the city of Nottingham, the former GCR/GNR Victoria station gradually became redundant as its services were withdrawn or diverted from the 1950s onwards. It suffered the ignominy of becoming an unstaffed halt before its final closure in July 1967. Only its clock tower remains today, dwarfed by a rather unattractive shopping centre on the prime city centre site. The former Midland station in Nottingham was more fortunate: it absorbed services from the ex-GNR Grantham line as well as handling traffic to and from Newark, Sheffield, Derby and Leicester. Meanwhile the former GNR terminus at London Road Low Level survived as a parcels depot long after its closure to passengers and has now been tastefully converted into a health club.

The 1960s saw some railway growth as well as cutbacks, particularly thanks to the coal industry, which was developing new seams on the eastern fringe of the coalfield to replace worked-out sites further west. BR built new branch lines to serve Cotgrave and Bevercotes pits, as well as adopting the 'merry-go-round' system to transport coal from pits to power stations with unprecedented efficiency. On the East Coast Main Line, BR replaced the flat crossing at Retford with a new dive-under line, eliminating the conflict between East Coast expresses and frequent coal trains to West Burton and Cottam Power Stations.

During the 1970s and 1980s the freight-only network in Nottinghamshire contracted as pits closed and as general freight traffic declined. In the Mansfield area the duplicate former MR branch lines to Rufford and Clipstone pits closed, while new infrastructure at Kirkby-in-Ashfield and at Shirebrook enabled BR to eliminate a busy level crossing on the former MR line at Kirkby and abandon the former GCR line through Shirebrook North. On the eastern side of the county, the little-used Bottesford to Newark line was a natural target for closure as it carried only one freight service, and that could easily be diverted via Grantham.

The main development of the 1990s was the staged re-opening of the 'Robin Hood Line' from Nottingham to Hucknall, Mansfield and Worksop. Most of the track had remained in use since the 1960s for coal traffic, but the re-opening involved digging out the abandoned ex-MR Kirkby Tunnel under the Robin Hood Hills. That work was complemented by the opening of Nottingham Express Transit, using a combination of railway and road alignments to bring 21st-century trams to the city and its northern suburbs.

The 'present' views in this album show the usual mixture of dereliction and redevelopment as well as a good number of thriving contemporary railway scenes. While it is sad to visit the sites of long-lost stations and yards, at least some former lines are accessible to the public as footpaths and cycle tracks, notable examples being the Southwell trail and the Newark-Cotham cycle route. And in the south of the county Ruddington is the base for an expanding heritage railway operation that hopes one day to link up with the Great Central Railway at Loughborough.

Thanks are due to the many photographers and owners of photographic collections who allowed the use of their material in this book. I am particularly grateful to David Holmes and Richard Casserley for their help with the captions.

Paul Shannon
Chester

BIBLIOGRAPHY

ABC British Railways Locomotives, combined volumes, various years (Ian Allan)
Allen, D. and Woolstenholmes, C. J. *A Pictorial Survey of Railway Signalling* (OPC)
Anderson, P. Howard *Forgotten Railways: The East Midlands* (David & Charles)
Baker, S. K. *Rail Atlas of Great Britain and Ireland*, various editions (OPC)
British Rail Track Diagrams: London Midland Region and Eastern Region (Quail Map Company)
British Railways Pre-Grouping Atlas and Gazetteer (Ian Allan)
Munns, R. T. *Milk Churns to Merry-go-round* (David & Charles)
Rhodes, Michael and Shannon, Paul *Freight Only Yearbook*, Nos 1 and 2 (Silver Link Publishing)
Rhodes, Michael *British Marshalling Yards* (OPC)
Shannon, Paul *ABC Railway Freight Operations* (Ian Allan)
Smith, Brian W. *Further Chapters in the History of an Estate Village*

Back issues of:
Branch Line News
Modern Railways
Rail Enthusiast/Rail
The Railway Magazine
The Railway Observer
Railway World

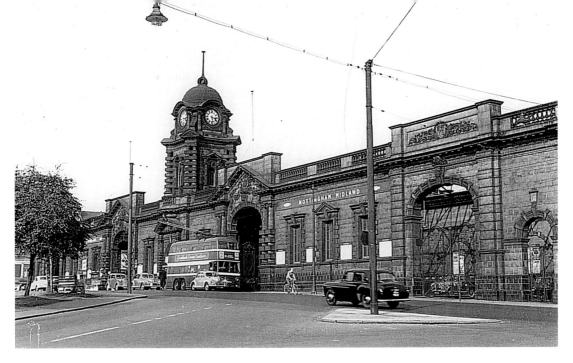

Central Nottingham

NOTTINGHAM MIDLAND: The first main-line railway to reach Nottingham was the Midland Counties Railway (MCR) from Derby, which opened in 1839 and ended at a terminus on the west side of Carrington Street. The MCR was soon amalgamated into the Midland Railway and, as the network of Midland lines around Nottingham grew, the terminus was replaced by a through station on the east side of Carrington Street. The combination of further traffic growth and competition from the new Great Central line prompted the Midland to open a new station on the same site in 1904, destined to survive into the 21st century as Nottingham's only main-line station. The trolleybus is an interesting feature of this exterior view dated 27 September 1959.

Nottingham lost its trolleybuses in 1966, but the former Midland Railway station retains its grand Edwardian frontage on Carrington Street, as pictured on 31 August 2005. *H. C. Casserley/PDS*

NOTTINGHAM MIDLAND: Former Midland Railway Class 2P 4-4-0 No 40454 prepares to depart from Nottingham Midland with the 6.35pm Mansfield train on 25 June 1949.

Some 57 years later, on 30 June 2006, the same platforms, footbridge, awnings and staircase remain in place, but the middle track has been removed to accommodate a servicing point. Central Trains Unit No 156414 departs with the 1640 service from Lincoln Central to Leicester, while unit No 170109 waits to form the 1726 departure to Worksop. *John Edgington/PDS*

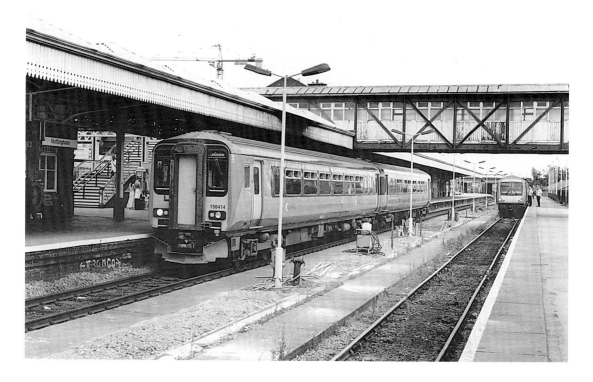

NOTTINGHAM MIDLAND: This fascinating panorama shows the approach to Nottingham Midland station from the east. The Midland Railway signal box overlooks London Road Junction, with the line to Melton Mowbray curving round to the right and Eastcroft sidings lying directly behind the box. On the left is the former GNR London Road Low Level terminus.

The same view is instantly recognisable on 30 June 2006, although the trackwork has been drastically reduced. No 66126 heads west with 6V31, the 1607 empty 'merry-go-round' train from Immingham to Margam, having carried a consignment of Welsh coal to the Coal Products Limited briquetting plant at Immingham. Eastcroft sidings now house a servicing facility for Central Trains as well as stabling for engineers' plant. *W. Taylor collection/PDS*

NOTTINGHAM MIDLAND: The western approach to Nottingham is pictured on 3 August 1984, with Class 43 power car No 43089 leading the 1500 departure to London St Pancras out of the station. The former goods and grain warehouse was no longer in railway use but still formed an attractive, if terminally decaying, feature in the scene.

The operational railway at this location has changed little in the last two decades, but the spare land on both sides of the railway has been put to more productive use. Although the train operator Midland Mainline retains a fleet of InterCity 125 units, it has also introduced Class 222 'Meridians' on many services. A four-car 'Meridian' unit forms the 1252 departure to London St Pancras on 2 July 2005. *Both PDS*

NOTTINGHAM MIDLAND SHED: Class 2P 4-4-0 No 40493 poses outside the former Midland Railway shed at Nottingham on 22 June 1952. Around this time the shed had an allocation of some 140 locomotives, representing more than a dozen different types.

The run-down of steam spelled the end for Nottingham shed as British Rail developed Toton instead as its main diesel depot for the East Midlands. The locomotive allocation at Nottingham fell sharply in the early 1960s and closure took place in 1965, after which the site was swallowed up by commercial development. The distant outline of Nottingham Castle, now a museum and art gallery, provides the only link with the past in this view dated 31 August 2005. *B. K. Green, Initial Photographics/PDS*

NOTTINGHAM LONDON ROAD LOW LEVEL was opened by the Great Northern Railway in 1857 as the terminus of its branch from Grantham. It lost its importance in 1900 when the GNR opened its link from Trent Lane Junction to Weekday Cross Junction, giving direct access to the joint GCR/GNR Victoria station. The Low Level station closed to passengers in 1944 but remained in use for parcels, its grand frontage with vigorous stone embellishments and projecting porte-cochère surviving as a reminder of its short-lived heyday. A solitary van adds life to this scene dated 31 May 1960.

The parcels traffic at London Road ceased in 1981 and, although severely damaged by a fire in the late 1990s, the Grade 2-listed building was restored and converted to the Holmes Place Health Club. The high quality of the restoration work is clearly seen in this view of 31 August 2005. *John Edgington/PDS*

SNEINTON: The MR and GNR built separate approaches to Nottingham from the east, terminating at Midland and London Road Low Level stations respectively. The MR line ran at a lower level than that of the GNR and included two level crossings; nevertheless it was the line that BR retained when it finally concentrated all traffic on to a single route by building a new connection at Carlton & Netherfield in 1965. A Swindon Class 120 unit passes the ex-MR gate box at Sneinton with the 0907 Birmingham New Street to Lincoln St Marks service on 27 July 1984. In the distance, above the last carriage, is the trainshed of London Road Low Level station, still in use for parcels traffic at that time.

The footbridge at Sneinton has been demolished, so the 'present' view of 2 July 2005 is taken from the crossing, which has been closed to motor vehicles since 1992. The box controls Colwick crossing by closed-circuit television as well as its own Meadow Lane crossing. *Both PDS*

A close-up of the refurbished Low Level trainshed on 31 August 2005, now part of the Holmes Place Health Club. *PDS*

NOTTINGHAM LONDON ROAD HIGH LEVEL, on the GNR spur between Trent Lane Junction and Weekday Cross Junction, was architecturally plain compared with its Low Level neighbour, but it became a far busier place as the GNR made the most of its access to Nottingham Victoria. The ground-level frontage and forecourt are pictured on 9 June 1956, with the platforms on the viaduct behind. The posters on the right advertise seaside trips to Blackpool, Boston and Skegness.

The High Level station closed to passengers in 1967 when trains from Grantham were finally diverted into Nottingham Midland. The station building became a furniture store and later Hooters bar, which we see illustrated on 31 August 2005. A section of the disused GNR viaduct is visible on the left.

Even the 'present' photographs in a book such as this can quickly pass into history: a return visit to Nottingham on 30 June 2006 found that the former High Level buildings had been demolished, together with the remaining stub of the long-disused viaduct. *H. C. Casserley/PDS (2)*

WEEKDAY CROSS JUNCTION was the meeting place of the GNR line from Grantham and the GCR main line. Both lines were carried on viaducts, enabling the railway to gain height on the approach to Victoria Street Tunnel and Victoria station. A quiet moment at Weekday Cross is captured in this photograph looking south on Saturday 9 June 1956.

Although the line north of Weekday Cross closed in 1968, both routes south of the junction remained in use until 1974 for freight trains to and from Ruddington and East Leake, which would run round just north of the junction. The GCR viaduct remained in place until the 1990s, but was then demolished to allow the first phase of Nottingham Express Transit to reach its Station Street terminus. A tram has just set out for Phoenix Park on 31 August 2005. *H. C. Casserley/PDS*

NOTTINGHAM VICTORIA: The centrepiece of Victoria was its imposing clock tower, standing proudly above the station's elegant Jacobean-style frontage. In contrast to its Midland Railway counterpart, Victoria was situated in the heart of the city and its construction at the end of the 19th century required the demolition of some 1,300 dwellings and 20 public houses. This early-20th-century postcard also shows one of Nottingham's first electric tram routes, part of a network that covered more than 25 miles by 1925.

When Victoria station was demolished, only the clock tower survived, but its ornate balconies and splendid dome and cupola seem sadly dwarfed by the concrete structures of the late 20th century in this view dated 31 August 2005. *J. K. Williams collection/PDS*

NOTTINGHAM VICTORIA presents a truly inter-regional scene, with London Midland traction and Southern Region stock on an Eastern Region main line, as Class 5 4-6-0 No 45208 of Low Moor shed (25F) leaves Victoria with a Bournemouth to York express in the summer of 1949. On the right is an LNER Class 'K2' 2-6-0. At this time Victoria was still busy with London-Manchester expresses, various cross-country workings and a range of local services, not to mention frequent freight trains.

The first significant service withdrawals on Great Central metals took place in the 1950s and the pace of decline hastened in the 1960s, as British Rail diverted long-distance traffic on to former Midland routes and abandoned the local services. However, the Bournemouth-York workings survived long enough to be dieselised and were not withdrawn until September 1966, when the line from Rugby to London Marylebone closed. After that Victoria handled only the DMU service to Rugby until the complete closure of the station in September 1967. The sandstone cutting and retaining wall confirm the correct location on 31 August 2005. *John Ward collection/PDS*

NOTTINGHAM VICTORIA: The massive engineering works required to build Victoria station are evident is this view on the northern approach dated 1 September 1966. Class 5 4-6-0 No 44984 has just emerged from the 1,200-yard Mansfield Road Tunnel into the 650-yard cutting that housed the station itself. A few days later the Bournemouth-York service would be withdrawn and the tunnel would become freight-only until the line closed completely in May 1968.

The 'present' view, dated 31 August 2005, is dominated by the multi-storey car park for the Victoria Centre. The skyline, too, has changed beyond recognition. *Roger Siviter/PDS*

NOTTINGHAM VICTORIA: BR Standard 9Fs were introduced to the Great Central main line in 1958 and became a common sight on freight services, especially the coal trains between Annesley and Woodford yards, which were dubbed 'windcutters' or 'runners' because of their speed. No 92068 enters Victoria station with a down train conveying mainly empty coal wagons on 22 August 1964.

Less than four years later, on 4 May 1968, a group of enthusiasts on a farewell tour of GNR lines around Nottingham take a last look at the station site before its redevelopment. British Rail was quick to realise the commercial potential of this prime city-centre location. *Paul Forbes/John Edgington*

Strictly speaking the 'present' equivalent of the earlier photographs would be a view of the basement car park, but this photograph of the Victoria Centre above it gives a fairer idea of the change in land use. Shoppers queue to take part in a competition on 31 August 2005. *PDS*

21

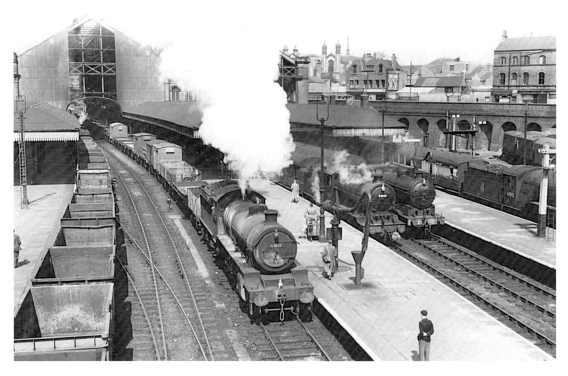

NOTTINGHAM VICTORIA: Our final view of Victoria station, dated April 1956, gives the clearest idea of its busy-ness before the rapid decline of the 1960s. The vantage point is Parliament Street bridge at the south end of the station. From left to right are: Class 'O1' 2-8-0 No 63630, dating back to 1918 but rebuilt by the LNER in 1945; Class 'J39' 0-6-0 No 64832, built in 1932; ex-GNR Class 'J6' 0-6-0 No 64230, built in 1914; and Gresley Class 'V2' 2-6-2 No 60815.

The 'present' view of 31 August 2005 is taken from the opposite side of Parliament Street to show the entrance to the shops now standing on the site. Hopes have been expressed that the Great Central alignment here might see a railway revival by an extension of Nottingham Express Transit, but that would require demolition of the Victoria Centre and seems extremely unlikely in the current climate. *John Ward collection/PDS*

South Nottinghamshire

WIDMERPOOL lay on the Midland Railway's cut-off line from Melton Mowbray to Nottingham, opened in 1879 to enable the company's expresses between London and northern England to avoid reversal at Nottingham, as well as improving rail access from the iron-ore fields in Leicestershire and Rutland. Local traffic, however, was sparse and Widmerpool station closed to passengers as early as 1949. Passing the abandoned platforms on 15 August 1962 is Stanier Class 8F 2-8-0 No 48156 with a northbound freight.

After the line closed as a through route in 1968, the track between Melton Mowbray and Edwalton was retained as the Old Dalby test track, initially for the Advanced Passenger Train project and more recently for testing West Coast 'Pendolino' units. However, when the 'Pendolino' delivery programme ended, no further use was found for the line and its testing equipment was due to be removed. The 'present' photograph of 21 August 2005 shows the up platform still in position, as well as the roof of the main station building, now part of the Pullman pub, and the down platform waiting room, partly obscured by bushes. *David Holmes/PDS*

NOTTINGHAM GOODS SOUTH (GCR): Just south of the Queen's Walk goods complex on the south side of Nottingham at Wilford, an impressive bridge with three pairs of 112-foot lattice girders carried the GCR main line across the River Trent. Despite the expense of the river crossing, the line became quadruple track at this point, with Nottingham Goods South signal box sandwiched between the two pairs of running lines at the south end of the bridge. In this undated scene Class 'K3' 2-6-0 No 61845 heads south with the Cleethorpes fish train.

The bridge was demolished in the 1980s and the 'present' photograph of 31 August 2005 shows no trace of the former GCR main line. However, the trackbed south of this point, behind the photographer, is still intact and has been earmarked for Phase Two of Nottingham Express Transit. *John Ward collection/PDS*

RUDDINGTON: Stanier Class 4 2-6-4T No 42453 enters Ruddington station with the 1.00pm Leicester Central to Chesterfield Central train on 13 February 1963. The island platform was typical of smaller stations on the GCR's London Extension, avoiding the duplication of passenger and staff facilities.

The overgrown station site on 21 August 2005 belies the fact that the Great Central Railway (Nottingham) Limited now owns the trackbed and hopes to reinstate the line from its present base at the former Ruddington MoD depot (now Nottingham Heritage Centre) to the northern outskirts of Leicester. *David Holmes/PDS*

GOTHAM: The GCR built a short freight-only branch from Gotham Sidings on the main line to Gotham Goods. The very last train from the branch terminus crosses the Kingston-on-Soar road in Gotham village on 8 March 1963, headed by Class 'B1' 4-6-0 No 61024. After that date the truncated branch continued to serve the plaster works on the outskirts of Gotham, until that traffic ceased in January 1970.

The railway alignment at this point is now a pleasant footpath. Gotham Primary School provides a clear link between the two photographs, the 'present' version recorded on 21 August 2005. *David Holmes/PDS*

RUSHCLIFFE HALT: Although only a minor halt as far as the passenger railway was concerned, Rushcliffe was a busy freight location thanks to the adjacent Hotchley Hill gypsum works. Class 'K3' 2-6-0 No 61917 propels empty 16-ton and 21-ton mineral wagons into the works on 23 July 1962, forming the 1.07pm departure from Nottingham Queen's Walk.

Freight traffic to Hotchley Hill ceased in 1984 but resumed in 1999. Rushcliffe Halt also became the southern terminus of Great Central Railway (Nottingham) operations in 2003. Robert Stephenson & Hawthorns 0-6-0 saddle tank No 63 *Corby* arrives at Rushcliffe with an afternoon working from Ruddington on 21 August 2005. The long-term aim is to replace the missing bridge over the Midland main line at Loughborough and link up with the established Great Central Railway to Leicester. *David Holmes/PDS*

RUSHCLIFFE HALT: Class 'J39' 0-6-0 No 64818 sets back into Hotchley Hill sidings with the 1.07pm departure from Queen's Walk on 3 July 1962, conveying empty hopper wagons that were used to carry gypsum to Bletchington cement works as well as mineral wagons used on other flows – the main destinations being Tring, Hope and Penyffordd. In the distance is Hotchley Hill signal box, which was erected after the Second World War.

The line from Loughborough to Hotchley Hill was bought by the Great Central Railway (Nottingham) Limited before gypsum traffic resumed in 1998, with EWS paying an access charge to use it. No 66219 leaves the works with 6E76, the 1203 departure to Milford sidings, on 26 July 2001. The containers will be reloaded with gypsum from the flue gas desulphurisation plant at Drax. *David Holmes/PDS*

EAST LEAKE: 'Royal Scot' 4-6-0 No 46125 *3rd Carabinier* approaches the island platform at East Leake with the 12.25pm Saturdays-only train from Ramsgate to Derby Friargate on 23 June 1962. By this time the Great Central line was in sharp decline; local services between Leicester and Nottingham would be withdrawn in 1963 and Nottingham to Marylebone semi-fasts in 1966, with the closure of the line south of Rugby. However, East Leake was one of two intermediate stations between Leicester and Nottingham to survive until the line's closure to passengers in May 1969, the other survivor being Loughborough Central.

Fortunately the track between Loughborough and Ruddington was left in position after the end of freight services in 1984, enabling it to re-open as far as Hotchley Hill in 1998 without vast expenditure. It is reserved for trains of containerised desulphogypsum on weekdays but is also available for occasional weekend use by the Great Central Railway (Nottingham), extending beyond its usual terminus at Rushcliffe. The 'present' scene is dated 21 August 2005. *David Holmes/PDS*

BEESTON Freightliner terminal opened in 1969 on the site of a small marshalling yard. At first it was successful but its location in the middle of the country meant that the potential for long-distance traffic, especially to and from ports such as Felixstowe and Southampton, was poorer than terminals such as Manchester and Leeds. By the mid-1980s it handled only one daily service, a trip working to and from Birmingham Landor Street. Passing the terminal on 3 August 1984 is No 40194 with a westbound train of track panels.

Freightliner withdrew from Beeston in 1987 and the site has since been colonised by willow and birch. Unit No 170502 hurries past forming the 1336 Nottingham to Hereford service on 2 July 2005. *Both PDS*

BEESTON: Class 4F 0-6-0 No 44033, bearing a Nottingham (16A) shedplate, drifts through Beeston station on 7 January 1957 while a rake of empty unfitted mineral wagons tailed by an LMS-design brake-van stands on the adjacent Nottingham-bound track.

No 44033 was withdrawn in 1961, but the brake-van may possibly have lasted much longer, given that examples of that design were still in common use in the 1980s. Beeston station itself has changed little in the past 50 years; a visit on 17 December 2005 finds unit No 158862 calling as the 0945 Cardiff Central to Nottingham service, while a Class 222 'Meridian' unit forms the 1252 service from Nottingham to London St Pancras. *Milepost 92½ (H. B. Priestley)/PDS*

ATTENBOROUGH: Fowler Class 4 2-6-4T No 42336 calls at Attenborough with a local service from Nottingham on 7 January 1957, while Stanier 8F No 48282 recedes light engine in the opposite direction.

The station buildings have disappeared and the platforms have been reduced in length, while residential development has taken place on both sides of the line. Unit No 170103 calls as the 1300 service from Nottingham to Cardiff Central on 17 December 2005. *Milepost 92½ (H. B. Priestley)/PDS*

KINGSTON-ON-SOAR: Officially known as Lord Belper's Mineral Railway, the 3-mile line from Kegworth to Kingston-on-Soar gypsum mine was completed in 1883. It was worked by horses in its early days but was later home to several 0-4-0 saddle tanks, including *Lady Angela*, which was purchased from Peckett in 1926. In this photograph dated 10 December 1962 *Lady Angela* negotiates one of the four level crossings on the branch with empty mineral wagons for the mine. At that time there were two scheduled workings each day from Kegworth to Kingston and back, with a weekly payload of 2,000 tons of crushed gypsum and plaster.

In 1963 the arrival of a Ruston & Hornsby diesel would spell the end for everyday steam on the branch, but *Lady Angela* remained on standby and saw occasional use on enthusiasts' specials right up to the line's closure in 1970. *Lady Angela* was sold to the Midland Railway Society at Shackerstone in 1971 and later moved to the Dart Valley Railway at Buckfastleigh, where she has recently been restored to full working order. The site of the crossing is pictured on 17 December 2005. *David Holmes/PDS*

Erewash Valley

TOTON: The up yard at Toton was substantially remodelled in 1948-50, with a mechanised hump and 37 sorting sidings divided into two sections: West Yard next to the main line and East Yard on the eastern side of the wagon repair shops. 'Peak' No 45064 leaves East Yard with 8V26, the 1551 departure to Acton, on 3 June 1981, conveying coal for Luton Limbury Road, Neasden and other depots in the London area.

The miners' strike of 1984/85 exacerbated the reduction in wagonload traffic as the railway concentrated as much coal as possible into 'merry-go-round' trainloads. East Yard closed completely and the site has returned to nature, the lighting masts now seeming strangely out of place in a small forest of birch, willow and hawthorn. The 'present' view is dated 31 August 2005. *Both PDS*

TOTON: Pairs of Class 20s were a characteristic sight on East Midlands coal trains in the 1970s and '80s, until replaced by the more powerful Classes 56 and 58. Nos 20196 and 20016 head north on the down high-level goods line past Toton Old Bank sidings with a rake of HTV hopper wagons on 3 June 1981. On the far left are the arrival lines for the up hump yard, still in use at that time.

Some 24 years later, on 7 June 2005, Freightliner Heavy Haul No 66554 heads south on the up main with loaded HHA hoppers. Old Bank sidings contain mainly infrastructure wagons, but on the left is a trainload of MEA wagons with coal for Ketton, flanked by a rake of hooded steel wagons allocated to the Boston-Wolverhampton circuit. *Both PDS*

TOTON: Nearly new Fowler Class 7F 0-8-0 No 9531 departs from Toton with an up coal train in August 1931. By this date Toton boasted more than 65 miles of sidings and was the main focus for LMS coal traffic in the Erewash Valley, a role that would become strengthened in BR days as the former LNER yards at Annesley and Colwick were run down.

The same location is easily recognisable nearly 74 years later on 7 June 2005. The semaphore signals and signal box are long gone and the up yard has been lifted, but the wagon repair depot in the middle distance still stands, albeit now disused, and the track layout in the foreground has changed little. No 66070 departs with a mixture of YEA, MCA and MDA infrastructure wagons, forming the 1512 service to Crewe. *R. S. Carpenter collection/PDS*

STANTON GATE: At least four engines are in steam in this characteristically busy scene at Stanton Gate, recorded just before the outbreak of the Second World War. Closest to the camera is Stanier 8F 2-8-0 No 8058 with empty wooden-bodied mineral wagons, while on the left a loaded train of similar wagons heads south. The sidings on the right handled traffic to and from Stanton Ironworks, then the biggest employer in the area and a major source of rail freight. The wagons on the far right would have carried coke to Stanton's blast furnaces.

   Resignalling and track remodelling transformed the scene at Stanton Gate during BR years, but an era has come and gone between the two photographs: the lighting masts and the shunting frame on the far right of the picture now stand disused. However, a single track – immediately to the left of the speed restriction sign – still gives access to the Stanton works and has been used from time to time by trainloads of pipes for export. The main line normally sees little passenger activity, but on 17 December 2005 a Virgin 'Voyager' unit is pictured heading south with a diverted service. *Lens of Sutton/PDS*

TROWELL station marked the divergence of the spur to Radford Junction from the main Erewash Valley line. Stanier 8F 2-8-0 No 48604 heads an up mineral train on the main line towards Toton in the late 1950s. Roughly 50 Stanier 8Fs were allocated to Toton depot at that time, with further examples based at other nearby sheds including Kirkby-in-Ashfield, Mansfield, Nottingham, Derby, Westhouses and Hasland.

The local service on the Erewash Valley line was targeted for withdrawal in the Beeching Report, and Trowell station duly closed in 1967. Since then all the sidings have gone and the down goods line has been taken out of use, leaving just the up and down main lines and the up goods line in operation. The lattice footbridge just beyond the former station is an interesting relic. Unit No 170634 heads south forming the 1552 Liverpool Lime Street to Norwich service on 7 June 2005. *R. S. Carpenter collection/PDS*

BENNERLEY: The 1,400-foot wrought-iron viaduct that once carried the Great Northern line to Derby Friargate over the Erewash Valley (see also *British Railways Past and Present* No 56) is eclipsed by the prefabricated loading bunker of Bennerley opencast disposal point, as No 56114 *Maltby Colliery* enters the sidings with 6Z72, the 0830 departure from Wardley, on 28 August 1992. The coal from Wardley would be blended at Bennerley before final delivery to one of the Trent Valley power stations.

The opencast loading bunker had a relatively short life and its demolition has opened up a clearer view of the viaduct, which, although disused since 1968, is now classed as a Grade 2-listed building and therefore protected for the foreseeable future. An infrastructure train heads south behind No 66165 on 1 September 2005. *Both PDS*

LANGLEY MILL: Stanier 8F 2-8-0 No 8195 heads south near Langley Mill with an assortment of wooden-bodied coal wagons on 7 May 1946. The wagons are likely to be destined for marshalling at Toton, and it will probably be several days before some of them reach their destination. With very few exceptions the standard unit of rail freight in those days was the single wagonload.

Today roughly 99% of rail-borne coal traffic moves in whole trainloads from loading point to destination. Operations were revolutionised by the launch of the 'merry-go-round' system in the 1960s, and today's higher-capacity bogie wagons have made the movement of coal by rail even more efficient. Freightliner Heavy Haul locomotive No 66555 heads south with imported coal for Rugeley Power Station on 1 September 2005. *H. C. Casserley/PDS*

LANGLEY MILL: Class 2P 4-4-0 No 383 calls at Langley Mill & Eastwood station with the 2.30pm Nottingham to Chesterfield service on 27 June 1933. The locomotive survived long enough to become BR No 40383, but the class became extinct in 1952.

The original Langley Mill & Eastwood station closed in 1967, but a new halt slightly further south of the original site was opened in 1986, funded jointly by Derbyshire County Council, Nottingham County Council, Amber Valley District Council and five parish councils. Unit No 170106 calls for custom while working the 1357 Norwich to Liverpool Lime Street service on 1 September 2005. *H. C. Casserley/PDS*

KIMBERLEY was one of the more important intermediate stations on the Great Northern line from Nottingham to Derby Friargate. It was also the junction for the GNR branch to Pinxton. Class 'L1' 2-6-4T stands at the westbound platform with the 2.5pm Nottingham Victoria to Derby Friargate train on 14 February 1962.

Kimberley station closed in 1964 when BR withdrew the service to Derby Friargate, all through traffic between Nottingham and Derby being diverted via the Midland route. The two 'present' photographs, taken on 17 December 2005, show how commercial development has encroached on part of the station site but left some undeveloped land for the 'Kimberley nature area', its railway origins recalled by the BR 'totem' sign. *David Holmes/PDS*

KIMBERLEY: Class 'O1' 2-8-0 No 63578 passes a Great Northern somersault signal as it approaches Kimberley station with an eastbound mineral train on 14 February 1962. This was a busy freight route with coal from numerous pits and heavy iron-ore trains to Stanton Ironworks, the latter having to negotiate the 1 in 100 climb out of the Leen Valley towards Kimberley.

The line from Derby Friargate closed completely in 1968, four years after the end of passenger services, and a small housing development has been squeezed into the narrow strip of land alongside the station approach road. Tenuous though it seems, a chimney stack on the far left of the 'past' photograph provides a link with the 'present' view recorded on 17 December 2005. *David Holmes/PDS*

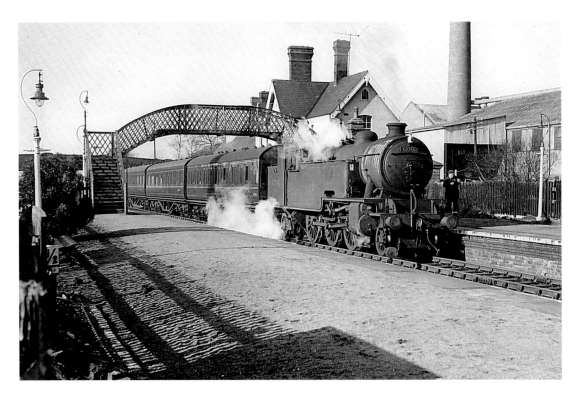

NEWTHORPE was the first station on the GNR branch to Pinxton, opened in 1875 to give the GNR a foothold in the rich Erewash Valley coalfield. Class 'L1' 2-6-4T No 67746 calls with the 1.12pm Pinxton to Nottingham Victoria train on 14 February 1962.

Passenger services on the Pinxton branch were withdrawn in January 1963, with goods services cut back to Eastwood at the same time. Final closure of the truncated branch took place in 1966. A 3-mile stretch of the alignment between Newthorpe and Eastwood was used for the A610 dual-carriageway, but the site of Newthorpe station is now occupied by industrial development, as pictured on 2 July 2005. *David Holmes/PDS*

PYE HILL & SOMERCOTES: No 67746 is seen again, pausing briefly for custom with the 4.15pm service from Nottingham Victoria to Pinxton on 19 February 1960. Among the many features of this scene that have slipped into history is the porter pulling the barrow-load of parcels.

The Pinxton branch suffered from mining subsidence in later years and BR abandoned the Eastwood-Pinxton stretch, including Pye Hill station, in 1963. A visit to the location on 2 July 2005 found the trackbed filled with colliery waste, although there were still traces of the road overbridge next to the station. *Milepost 92½ (H. B. Priestley)/PDS*

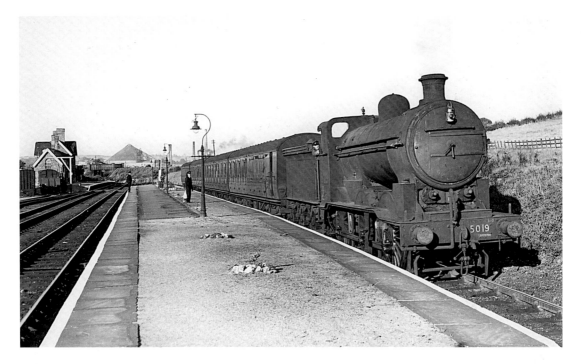

PINXTON SOUTH: Although intended mainly for colliery traffic, the GNR Pinxton branch carried a regular passenger service from 1876 until 1963. The terminus at Pinxton South boasted three platforms and a substantial station building; until about 1906 Pinxton even had its own two-road locomotive shed. GNR Class 'J2' 0-6-0 No 5019 awaits departure with the 6.55pm service to Nottingham Victoria on 13 May 1949. Just to the right of the station building is the bridge that carried a short extension of the GNR branch over the Midland line to reach Langton Colliery.

Careful study of large-scale maps was necessary to locate the former station site on 1 September 2005. *John Edgington/PDS*

Leen Valley

NEW BASFORD: The opening of the joint GCR/GNR Nottingham Victoria station and of the GCR main line through the Leen Valley provided a shorter route for Great Northern trains from Nottingham to Derby, Pinxton and Shirebrook, which had previously been routed either via Gedling or via the Nottingham Suburban Railway. Entering New Basford station on 22 July 1961 is Ivatt Class 4 2-6-0 No 43152 with four LNER corridor carriages forming the 1215 service from Nottingham Victoria to Pinxton. On leaving New Basford the train will take the spur from Bagthorpe Junction to Basford North.

On 29 April 2006 the site of New Basford station is seen in the early stages of redevelopment. The houses on the right of the 'past' picture are now obscured by trees. *H. C. Casserley/PDS*

THORNEYWOOD: The Nottingham Suburban Railway from Trent Lane Junction to Daybrook opened in 1889 and was the first attempt to provide a more direct route for GNR trains heading north from Nottingham. It became largely redundant after the GCR main line opened in 1899; its three intermediate stations at Thorneywood, St Ann's Well and Sherwood closed as early as 1916 and through passenger services via the Suburban Railway ended in 1931. The section south of Thorneywood then closed completely, leaving a goods-only branch from Daybrook to Thorneywood to serve three local brickworks until 1951. The two 'past' photographs record the visit of a Railway Correspondence & Travel Society railtour to Thorneywood on 16 June 1951, hauled by Class 'C12' 4-4-2T No 67363.

Although much of the Suburban Railway route is difficult to trace today, the bricked-up tunnel portal at Thorneywood provides a reminder of this little-known line. The 'present' photograph is dated **31 August 2005.** *A. G. Forsyth, Initial Photographics/PDS*

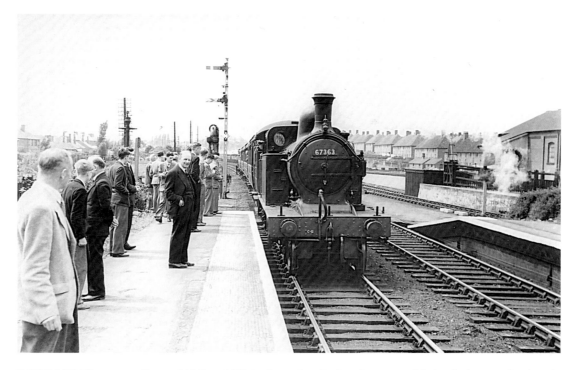

DAYBROOK: The same railtour of 16 June 1951 is pictured at Daybrook, presumably just before or after its trip to Thorneywood. At that time the line through Daybrook would still have been busy with goods traffic, especially to and from Colwick yard, but it was very much a secondary route as far as passengers were concerned.

Daybrook station closed to passengers in 1960 and to goods in 1964, while the line between Gedling and Daybrook was closed to all traffic in 1960 because of mining subsidence in Mapperley Tunnel. No trace of the station survives today, as pictured on 25 July 2005. *A. G. Forsyth, Initial Photographics/PDS*

BAGTHORPE: Class 'K3' 2-6-0 No 61938 hurries south on the Great Central main line towards Bagthorpe Junction with the 2.20pm Sheffield Victoria to Nottingham Victoria semi-fast train on 24 July 1957. The Great Central main line would be transferred from Eastern Region to London Midland Region control in the following year and its days as a major express route would soon be over.

As with a number of pairings in this volume, the houses on the skyline of the 'past' photograph are still present but frustratingly obscured by more modern development in the 'present' scene, recorded on 2 July 2005. *David Holmes/PDS*

BASFORD NORTH: Class 'J6' 0-6-0 No 64215 has just set out from Basford North with the 4.17pm local train to Nottingham Victoria via Gedling on 24 July 1957. There were railways on three levels here: the train is just about to pass under the Great Central main line at right angles, while the track curving round on the right passed under both lines and joined the Great Central main line at Bagthorpe Junction.

The closure of all lines at this location by 1968 paved the way for earthworks on a large scale, removing all traces of the former railway alignments. Housing estates occupy much of the land, but a welcome green space is pictured on 2 July 2005. *David Holmes/PDS*

BASFORD NORTH: Class 'B1' 4-6-0 No 1171, built only the previous month, approaches Basford & Bulwell station with seven assorted pre-Grouping compartment carriages forming the 12.50 Grantham to Derby service on 12 July 1947. The line curving round to the left connected with the Great Central main line just south of Bulwell Common station.

Basford & Bulwell was renamed Basford North in 1953 to reduce the confusion with other local stations having Basford or Bulwell in their names. The station closed to passengers in 1964 and to goods in 1967; through mineral traffic ceased in 1968 and the railway formation was then free for redevelopment. A bleak industrial estate occupies the site today, as pictured on 2 July 2005. *H. C. Casserley/PDS*

RADFORD: Stanier 8F 2-8-0 No 48282 passes through Radford station with a coal train from the Leen Valley on 5 November 1956. Curving round to the left is the line to Trowell, used by expresses on the former Midland Railway route between Sheffield and Nottingham.

Freight at Radford is now virtually non-existent, but both routes carry a regular passenger service. The junction retains the same track layout as 50 years ago, although the signalling is now controlled from Trent power box. Unit No 158788 forms the 0952 Liverpool Lime Street to Norwich service on 2 July 2005. *Milepost 92½ (H. B. Priestley)/PDS*

BASFORD VERNON was the first station beyond Radford Junction on the Midland line to Mansfield; the suffix 'Vernon' was added in the early 1950s to distinguish the station from Basford North on the Great Northern line. Stanier 8F 2-8-0 No 48097 heads south with a coal train on 23 February 1959.

Basford Vernon station closed to passengers less than a year after the date of the 'past' photograph, presumably as a result of competition from buses, and the line became freight-only in 1964. In recent years the coal traffic has ceased, but the route has undergone a double renaissance for passengers – first the 'heavy rail' 'Robin Hood Line' revival from 1993 onwards, then the launch of Nottingham Express Transit in March 2004. A tram bound for Station Street pulls away from the Basford stop on 17 December 2005. *Milepost 92½ (H. B. Priestley)/PDS*

LINCOLN STREET CROSSING: Period road vehicles and 'HALT' signs add nostalgic flavour to this view of Lincoln Street Crossing, just north of Basford station, in early 1960. The viaduct in the distance carried the GNR line to Derby Friargate over the Leen Valley.

The second photograph, taken with a slightly longer lens, shows the location in its freight-only period. Nos 20147 and 20183 approach the crossing with a vacuum-braked coal train from Bestwood Park sidings to Toton on 14 April 1983.

The third view, dated 17 December 2005, had to be taken from a lower angle because the footbridge that provided the vantage point for the earlier photographs was out of use awaiting demolition. With the re-opened 'Robin Hood Line' barely visible behind the fence on the right, a tram sets out from the David Lane stop. Lincoln Street signal box closed in 2001 and was moved to Leicester for use as a training facility. *W. Taylor collection/PDS (2)*

BULWELL MARKET: Stanier Class 3MT 2-6-2T No 40168 calls at the former Midland Railway station in Bulwell with the 5.31pm train from Worksop to Nottingham Midland on 23 July 1960.

The 'heavy rail' route beyond Lincoln Street was singled to allow the sharing of the trackbed with Nottingham Express Transit. A new station was provided at Bulwell in 1994, later offering interchange with Nottingham Express Transit over the footbridge. Unit No 156413 calls with the 1540 service from Worksop to Nottingham on 2 July 2005. Although the station is unstaffed, an electronic display gives useful real-time train service information. *David Holmes/PDS*

BULWELL COMMON: Three railway routes once ran parallel through Bulwell – a case of wasteful duplication if ever there was one! The Great Northern line closed to passengers as early as 1931, while the Great Central and Midland lines retained local passenger services until 1963 and 1964 respectively. Goods traffic continued on all three routes into the 1960s. Passing the former GCR Bulwell Common station on the afternoon of 13 February 1963 is Class 'O1' 2-8-0 No 63594 with unfitted coal empties.

After closure in 1966 the railway formation was quickly released for housing development. However, the road overbridge survives to allow this elevated view of the former station site on 2 July 2005. *David Holmes/PDS*

BESTWOOD PARK sidings remained active as a gathering point for non-'merry-go-round' coal traffic in the Leen Valley until the 1980s. Several rakes of vacuum-braked HTV hopper wagons can be seen in the sidings as No 47195 heads south with the 6T54 'mgr' train from Newstead to Ratcliffe on 14 April 1983. At that time the Leen Valley line served five collieries: Babbington, Calverton, Hucknall, Linby and Newstead.

One by one, the remaining collieries closed, with just Calverton surviving until 1999. The view from the bridge at Bestwood Park has changed almost beyond recognition in the last two decades, with the 'Robin Hood' and Nottingham Express Transit lines now running side by side. Unit No 150132 forms the 1637 Mansfield Woodhouse to Nottingham service on 2 July 2005. *Both PDS*

HUCKNALL pit was sunk in 1861 and was the first major colliery in the Leen Valley. It was reconstructed between 1957 and 1969 to give access to lower seams, and was later equipped with a rapid loading bunker for 'merry-go-round' trains. On 14 April 1983 No 47364 passes Hucknall with an 'mgr' train from Newstead to Ratcliffe. In the left-hand sidings are coal wagons of an earlier vintage – railway-owned MCV minerals and wooden-bodied National Coal Board stock.

The last coal from Hucknall was brought to the surface in October 1986 following the appearance of a massive sandstone intrusion in the main seam. The pit was quickly dismantled and the land offered for redevelopment. Tramway and railway run side by side past the site of Hucknall Colliery today; unit No 156414 is pictured on a Nottingham-bound working on 25 July 2005. *Both PDS*

HUCKNALL TOWN: Class 'O1' 2-8-0 No 63578 heads north through the long-closed ex-GNR Hucknall Town station with empty mineral wagons on 14 February 1962 – the same locomotive and train as were pictured half an hour previously at Kimberley (page 44). The ex-MR and ex-GNR lines ran very close to each other at this point, with Hucknall Colliery sandwiched between them.

No trace remains today of the former GNR station, and a supermarket has been built on the trackbed. However, the adjacent ex-MR station, reached by the same access road as the supermarket, is enjoying a double revival thanks to Nottingham Express Transit and the 'Robin Hood Line' (see page 6). *David Holmes/PDS*

LINBY (MR): The mining village of Linby originally had two passenger stations, one on the Midland and the other on the Great Northern line. Even before the Grouping this was found to be excessive, and the Great Northern station closed in 1916. Stanier Class 4 2-6-4T No 42588 calls at the former Midland station with an afternoon train to Nottingham on 3 October 1964. The down platform was located on the other side of the crossing, behind the photographer. The Midland and Great Northern lines ran parallel at this point, while the Great Central line crossed from one side of the valley to the other by the bridge seen on the skyline.

Linby station closed with the withdrawal of Leen Valley passenger services in 1964, and while the 'Robin Hood Line' project brought passenger trains back to the line in 1993, no station was provided at Linby. Unit No 156403 approaches the crossing with the 1040 Worksop to Nottingham train on 17 December 2005. *W. Taylor/PDS*

LINBY (GNR): The closure of Linby's GNR station in 1916 marked the start of a long period of decline for the Great Northern route in the Leen Valley. The line closed to passengers in 1931, to through freight in 1960 and to local colliery traffic in 1968. Remarkably the formation was still double-track on 13 February 1963 when Class 'O1' 2-8-0 No 63594 was photographed heading south with a brake-van near the station site. The full tender suggests that the locomotive may have just set out from Annesley shed.

A bridle path traces this section of the GNR line today, as pictured on 2 July 2005. *David Holmes/PDS*

ANNESLEY: The former Midland line was closed as a through route beyond Annesley in 1968. The northernmost section of the truncated line served Annesley and Newstead collieries, located less than half a mile apart. Coal from Annesley was brought to the surface at Bentinck from the early 1980s onwards, while Newstead dispatched coal by rail until 1983. With Annesley Colliery in the background No 47364 approaches Annesley box with 'merry-go-round' empties for Newstead on 14 April 1983. It will pull forward past the box before setting back into the sidings on the left.

The 'present' photograph, dated 17 December 2005, shows the derelict headstocks and other buildings of Annesley Colliery still standing, while the now passenger-only 'Robin Hood Line' runs across the foreground. The colliery site is soon to be redeveloped, but some of the buildings are likely to be retained because of their historical significance. *Both PDS*

Mansfield district

NEW HUCKNALL sidings lay on the Great Central main line between Kirkby Bentinck and Tibshelf stations. Class 'O1' 2-8-0 No 63773 heads south with an unfitted coal train in the late 1950s. In the distance is a line of wagons on the mineral line to New Hucknall Colliery.

This stretch of the Great Central main line lost its local passenger services in 1963 and closed to all except local colliery traffic in 1966. The site of New Hucknall sidings has been built over, but a path runs along the side of the former railway alignment, as pictured on 17 December 2005. *W. Taylor collection/PDS*

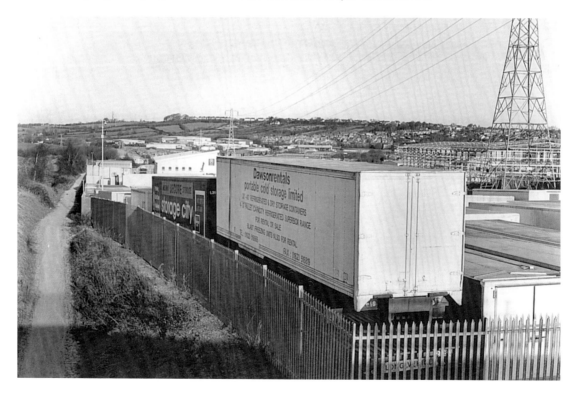

KIRKBY-IN-ASHFIELD EAST: Class 3P 4-4-2T No 41947 calls at the former Midland Railway station at Kirkby-in-Ashfield with the 4.40pm train from Nottingham to Whitwell on 2 September 1955. This locomotive type dated back to 1909; No 41947 was to remain in service until 1960 and was the last member of the class to be withdrawn.

The passenger service from Nottingham ended in 1964 but Kirkby-in-Ashfield station remained in use for another year for trains from Pye Bridge. After that the route from Pye Bridge remained busy with freight, but trains were diverted in 1972 over a re-laid stretch of the former GNR route through Kirkby-in-Ashfield and the Midland formation was abandoned. The 'present' view of 1 September 2005 shows the former station site now occupied by a hospital car park. *H. C. Casserley/PDS*

KIRKBY-IN-ASHFIELD SHED: The Midland Railway shed at Kirkby-in-Ashfield housed predominantly freight locomotives. This view, recorded in 1947, shows at least nine 2-8-0s and three 0-6-0s, types that would continue to dominate the depot's allocation until its closure to steam in 1966.

The shed was enlarged in 1958 by the addition of a two-road structure adjoining the original building. Confusingly, the shed changed its code twice during the BR period: it was 16C from 1948 to 1955, 16B from 1955 to 1963, and 16E from 1963 to 1966. After closure to steam it remained in use as a diesel stabling point for a few more years. The houses on Lowmoor Road confirm the correct location for the 'present' view dated 1 September 2005. *John Ward collection/PDS*

SUTTON-IN-ASHFIELD (MR): The Midland Railway opened its three-quarter-mile branch from Sutton Junction, on the Nottingham-Mansfield line, to Sutton-in-Ashfield in 1893. The branch soon lost much of its potential business as both the Great Northern and Great Central railways built their own lines through the centre of the town. The branch passenger service was withdrawn temporarily for two periods before nationalisation and was reduced to an unadvertised workmen's service in 1949; it was withdrawn completely in 1951. This view of the terminus shows Midland Railway Class 1P 0-4-4T No 1297 on the so-called 'Penny Emma' service to Sutton Junction on 2 August 1941.

No trace remains of the Midland Railway alignment in the town centre today. The use of a large-scale map was required to find the correct spot in Homebase car park on 1 September 2005. *H. C. Casserley/PDS*

SUTTON-IN-ASHFIELD TOWN: The Great Northern Railway opened its line from Kirkby-in-Ashfield to Langwith Junction in stages between 1897 and 1901. The most important intermediate station on the line was Sutton-in-Ashfield, where the GNR invested in a substantial street-level booking office and accommodation for passengers and staff on both platforms. In the first picture the station is pictured looking south shortly after it opened.

Passenger traffic over the GNR route failed to live up to expectations and local services were withdrawn in 1931. Sutton-in-Ashfield GNR station enjoyed a brief revival in 1956 when British Railways re-introduced a limited service on the GNR line following the withdrawal of passenger services on the Mansfield Railway. Our second photograph, dated 9 June 1956, shows Class 'A5' 4-6-2T No 69818 arriving at the recently re-opened station with the 1.15pm service from Nottingham Victoria.

The 1956 revival failed to attract sufficient business and the service was withdrawn again after just eight months. The line remained in use for excursion and freight traffic but was closed completely in 1968. The cutting has since been filled in, as pictured on 1 September 2005. *Lens of Sutton/ H. C. Casserley/PDS*

SKEGBY was the next intermediate station north of Sutton-in-Ashfield on the Great Northern line. Class 5 2-6-0 No 42897 departs with a special from Pleasley East to Dudley on 2 August 1959.

The former GNR line between Sutton-in-Ashfield and Pleasley now provides a pleasant traffic-free cycle route and footpath. The 'present' scene is dated 1 September 2005. *R. J. Buckley, Initial Photographics/PDS*

MANSFIELD TOWN: The Midland Railway reached Mansfield in the late 1840s but it was some time before the railway system around the town was fully developed: the Midland lines to Southwell and Worksop opened in 1871 and 1875 respectively and the GCR-worked Mansfield Railway from Kirkby-in-Ashfield to Clipstone opened in stages between 1913 and 1917. The Midland station frontage and hotel – originally a private house but purchased by the Midland Railway in 1862 – are pictured on 2 September 1955.

In October 1964 Mansfield acquired the dubious distinction of being the largest regional centre in England without a passenger station. It took another 31 years for passenger trains to return to the town with the extension of the 'Robin Hood Line' to Mansfield Woodhouse. Fortunately the station building at Mansfield was still intact and could be converted back to its original function, as illustrated on 1 September 2005. *H. C. Casserley/PDS*

MANSFIELD TOWN: Class 3F 0-6-0 No 43727 calls at Mansfield with the 3.40pm train from Worksop to Nottingham on 2 September 1955. At that time more than 300 examples of this class remained in British Railways stock; the last survivors were withdrawn in 1964.

Although Mansfield has lost its overall roof and original platforms, the largely intact buildings on the down platform make it hard to believe that the station was closed to passengers from 1964 until 1995. Single-car No 153365 calls as the 1326 Nottingham to Worksop service on 1 September 2005. *H. C. Casserley/PDS*

MANSFIELD WOODHOUSE: The former MR line through Mansfield was never an express passenger route, but summertime holiday trains provided some variety from the run-of-the-mill local services between Nottingham and Mansfield. Class 5 'Crab' 2-6-0 No 42756 calls at the station with the 11.24am Mablethorpe to Radford train on Sunday 23 June 1963.

Mansfield Woodhouse became the temporary terminus of the revived 'Robin Hood Line' in 1995. Initially trains terminated in the former goods shed, which is hidden behind the sign on the right in this photograph; the down platform was brought into use when the line was extended to Worksop in 1998. Unit No 158788 calls with the 1040 service from Worksop to Nottingham on 1 September 2005. *Milepost 92½ (H. B. Priestley)/PDS*

SHIREBROOK COLLIERY: The opening of Shirebrook colliery in 1896 transformed a rural village into a busy industrial town, its population rising tenfold between 1891 and 1901. The pit was extensively modernised from the 1950s onwards and was merged with Pleasley Colliery around 1980; however, it was targeted for closure by British Coal and wound its last coal in 1993. Trainload Coal-liveried No 58037 backs its 'merry-go-round' train under the rapid loading bunker at Shirebrook on 29 October 1992.

Since the colliery closed English Partnerships and the East Midlands Development Agency have managed the reclamation and redevelopment of the site for housing, small businesses and large-scale industrial units. Part of the development is pictured on 23 July 2005. *Both PDS*

SHIREBROOK WEST: Class 3 2-6-2T No 40089 departs from Shirebrook West with the 5.30pm train from Worksop to Nottingham Midland on 26 August 1961. The station had officially acquired its suffix 'West' in 1951 – an odd name since the station lies on the east side of the town.

Passenger services returned to Shirebrook in May 1998 when the 'Robin Hood Line' was extended from Mansfield Woodhouse to Worksop. Unit No 150237 forms the 1440 Worksop to Nottingham service on 23 July 2005. *David Holmes/PDS*

SHIREBROOK WEST: BR Standard Class 4 4-6-0 No 75062 is terminating at Shirebrook West with the 12.00 holiday train from Yarmouth Vauxhall on Saturday 26 August 1961. In a few minutes the platform will be thronging with miners and their families returning home after a welcome break by the seaside – few would have owned cars at that time.

Much has come and gone between the two photographs. Passenger services ended in 1964 but resumed in 1998, while the traction maintenance depot in the former goods yard was opened in the 1960s but abandoned in the 1990s. Unit No 150229 calls with the 1426 service from Nottingham to Worksop on 23 July 2005. *David Holmes/PDS*

SHIREBROOK JUNCTION: The curve between Shirebrook Junction and Warsop Junction allowed through running between the MR and GCR systems, a useful facility for excursions as well as goods traffic. Class 'B1' 4-6-0 No 61269 leaves Midland metals with a special from Chesterfield Midland to Skegness on 19 August 1951.

More than 50 years later, the signalling and track layout at Shirebrook Junction appear unchanged, although the curve in the foreground sees little use following the run-down of local collieries. Unit No 156401 forms the 0823 service from Nottingham to Worksop on 1 September 2005. *R. J. Buckley, Initial Photographics/PDS*

SHIREBROOK NORTH: Class 'B1' 4-6-0 No 61004 *Oryx* heads east from Shirebrook North with the 9.25am special from Clowne South to Skegness on 19 August 1951. The train is on the former GCR line to Clipstone and has just passed over the ex-MR Mansfield-Worksop line; some of the stabling sidings at Langwith Junction shed are visible on the left.

The bridge over the ex-MR line was taken out of use in 1974 and the ex-GCR line was diverted via a new north-facing curve to join the ex-MR line. By 2005 the curve was used only by infrequent trainloads of coal from Welbeck and Thoresby collieries, destined mainly for Cottam and West Burton power stations. The 'present' view is dated 1 September 2005. *R. J. Buckley, Initial Photographics/PDS*

SHIREBROOK NORTH: Class 'B1' 4-6-0 No 61153 reaches its journey's end at the rambling, decrepit Shirebrook North station on 26 August 1961. The train is the 5.25pm Saturdays-only departure from Nottingham Victoria. The running-in board on the left displays the name 'Shirebrook North for Langwith', which was adopted by the LNER in 1924 instead of Langwith Junction. The station had lost its regular all-year passenger services in 1955, but would continue to handle excursion traffic until 1964. The size of the station reflects the large number of routes that once converged on it, from Clipstone (GCR), Shirebrook West (MR), Kirkby-in-Ashfield (GNR), Chesterfield (GCR) and Beighton (GCR).

The railway through Shirebrook North ceased to be used as a through route after BR diverted the Clipstone line to join the ex-MR line to Worksop in 1974. The site is seen gradually returning to nature on 23 July 2005. *David Holmes/PDS*

LANGWITH: Situated just on the Derbyshire side of the Nottinghamshire/Derbyshire border, the village of Langwith grew up after the opening of Langwith Colliery in 1876. Its railway station opened around the same time, giving the village direct links to Worksop, Mansfield and Nottingham. On 26 August 1961 Stanier Class 3 2-6-2T No 40073 calls at Langwith with the 5.14pm from Nottingham Midland to Worksop.

While Langwith pit lasted until 1978, the station closed in 1964 with the withdrawal of the Nottingham-Worksop service. A new station named Langwith Whaley Thorns was opened in 1998 on a different site, adjacent to the former colliery. The location of the old station is pictured on 1 September 2005. *David Holmes/PDS*

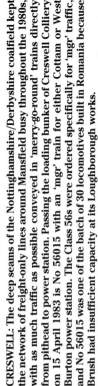

CRESWELL: The deep seams of the Nottinghamshire/Derbyshire coalfield kept the network of freight-only lines around Mansfield busy throughout the 1980s, with as much traffic as possible conveyed in 'merry-go-round' trains directly from pithead to power station. Passing the loading bunker of Creswell Colliery on 15 April 1983 is No 56015 with an 'mgr' train for either Cottam or West Burton power station. The Class 56s were ordered specifically for 'mgr' traffic, and No 56015 was one of the batch of 30 locomotives built in Romania because Brush had insufficient capacity at its Loughborough works.

Creswell Colliery closed in 1991 and the rapid loader was dismantled, leaving just an area of concrete beside the railway. Unit No 150237 forms the 1326 Nottingham to Worksop service on 23 July 2005. *Both PDS*

83

WARSOP was the first station east of Shirebrook on the Lancashire, Derbyshire & East Coast Railway (LD&ECR) line from Chesterfield to Lincoln, later part of the GCR. Ex-GNR Class 'C12' 4-4-2T No 4528 approaches Warsop with three former GCR coaches on 8 May 1946, forming the 4.00pm train from Chesterfield Market Place to Lincoln Central.

Warsop station closed to regular passenger services in 1955 and to excursion traffic in 1964, but the platforms and fencing were still in position on 1 September 2005. The outlook for this stretch of line is bleak as it now serves only two collieries, Thoresby and Welbeck, and a passenger revival is unlikely. *H. C. Casserley/PDS*

MANSFIELD CONCENTRATION SIDINGS were located on the former GCR-worked Mansfield Railway from Kirkby-in-Ashfield to Clipstone, which opened as late as 1916. As their name suggests, the sidings were a gathering point for coal from pits in the Mansfield area. On 15 June 1981 one of the yard pilots, No 08429, leaves the empty wagon sidings while No 56090 awaits its turn.

The Concentration Sidings became disused as wagonload coal traffic dried up and the site has since been colonised by broom and birch. The last revenue-earning traffic on the through lines was coal to Rufford stocking site in 2004. The disused tracks are pictured on 23 July 2005. *Both PDS*

BILSTHORPE: During the early 20th century the coal-mining industry migrated east to exploit the reserves under Sherwood Forest. The new pits required new branch lines, three of which diverged from the former Mansfield Railway at Clipstone to serve Rufford, Blidworth and Bilsthorpe. The Bilsthorpe pit began production in 1925, by which time the Mansfield Railway was part of the LNER. This view, dated 29 October 1992, shows No 58018 just about to run round its loaded train at Bilsthorpe before departing for West Burton Power Station.

Bilsthorpe wound its last coal in March 1997, and the 4½-mile branch closed shortly afterwards. The neighbouring pits at Rufford and Blidworth had already closed by then, although rail traffic to Rufford stocking site continued until 2004. The intact but overgrown run-round loop at Bilsthorpe is pictured on 1 September 2005. *Both PDS*

EDWINSTOWE: Although Edwinstowe was not a colliery village, its prosperity in the 20th century was closely linked to the sinking of new pits in the surrounding area. The station lost its regular passenger service in 1955 but, like Warsop, it continued to handle holiday traffic until 1964. It still looks well cared for in this photograph of 26 August 1961, showing Class 'K3' 2-6-0 No 61912 in charge of a westbound goods train.

The platforms and station building were still standing on 22 July 2005, as was the signal post – albeit now only with its Distant arm – at the end of the eastbound platform. *David Holmes/PDS*

OLLERTON Colliery began production in 1926. It was connected to the LNER (ex-GCR) line between Clipstone and Lincoln, and from 1931 it was also served by a joint LNER/LMS mineral line from Farnsfield Junction. No 31302 has just departed from Ollerton Colliery sidings on the ex-GCR line with the T19 trip working to Mansfield Concentration Sidings on 15 June 1981.

The axe fell on Ollerton Colliery in 1994 and its site was redeveloped as Sherwood Energy Village, providing the hope of employment for some former miners and their families. The former GCR line remained in use for nearly another decade for access to High Marnham Power Station, but by 23 July 2005 the tracks were heavily rusted and the box boarded up. A subsequent visit in 2006 found the box severely damaged by fire. *Both PDS*

FLEDBOROUGH: The former GCR line through the Dukeries formed a useful route for holiday trains between the Nottinghamshire coalfield and East Coast resorts. On 20 August 1960 Class 'K3' 2-6-0 No 61852 heads west near Fledborough with the 1.28pm Saturdays-only train from Cleethorpes to Nottingham Victoria. The train will continue its journey via the Mansfield Railway from Clipstone to Kirkby-in-Ashfield, then on the ex-GCR main line through the Leen Valley.

The line was severed as a through route beyond High Marnham in 1980. Today, with High Marnham Power Station closed, the remaining single track through Fledborough is gathering weeds, as seen on 23 July 2005. *David Holmes/PDS*

HIGH MARNHAM was one of several major coal-fired power stations that opened alongside the River Trent in the 1960s. The track layout at High Marnham was designed with traditional operations in mind – empty wagons on one side and loaded on the other – but in practice coal was received in 'merry-go-round' trainloads. On 12 April 1984 No 56117 arrives with 7G34 from Ollerton. In the distance, just above the Class 56, is a tantalising glimpse of No 37215 with a tracklifting train on the former through line to Lincoln.

Coal traffic to High Marnham ceased in March 2003, but the railway survived a little longer to remove surplus stockpiled coal. By 23 July 2005 almost all the track had been removed. *Both PDS*

East of Nottingham

NETHERFIELD is now the first station out of Nottingham on the former GNR Grantham line. Originally named Colwick, the station was subsequently known as Netherfield, Netherfield & Colwick and Netherfield Junction. The dilapidated buildings on the island platform, which presumably dated back to GNR days, were in the process of demolition on 22 July 1961.

The station became an unstaffed halt in 1968, and at the time of writing it has a sparse service of only six eastbound and five westbound trains each weekday. The rather bleak platform is pictured facing east on 31 August 2005. *H. C. Casserley/PDS*

COLWICK: The Great Northern Railway strengthened its presence in Nottingham with a major engine shed and marshalling yard complex at Colwick. At one time the shed had an allocation of 400 locomotives, and it survived into BR days, first as 38A and later 40E. Standing outside the 18-road shed building on 24 July 1955 is Class 'O4/7' 2-8-0 No 63699.

The shed closed to steam in December 1966 and lasted just a few more years as a diesel stabling point. Its 70-foot-high concrete coaling tower was demolished in 1971 and gradually the whole site was cleared, partly to make way for commercial development and partly for a new road, as pictured on 25 July 2005. *Brian Morrison/PDS*

COLWICK: 'Britannia' Class 7 4-6-2 No 70012 *John of Gaunt* passes Colwick East Junction with a Railway Correspondence & Travel Society special from Nottingham to Cleethorpes on 2 October 1965. This location was originally the junction for the GNR 'back line' to Gedling and Basford, but the expansion of Colwick marshalling yard forced the diversion of the 'back line' to a new junction further east on the Grantham line, known as Rectory Junction. The turnout in the foreground gave access to the Colwick Estates Railway, which remained in use until the 1980s.

Today the site of Colwick yard is part industrial estate and part wasteland, although a rail-served oil terminal survives on the north side of the former complex. Unit No 170502 passes the site of Colwick East Junction on 25 July 2005 with the 0852 Liverpool Lime Street to Norwich service – a journey scheduled to take 5 hours 18 minutes. *Paul Forbes/PDS*

GEDLING Colliery opened in 1903; it was conveniently located on the GNR 'back line' from Colwick to Basford and was within easy reach of Colwick yard. After the 'back line' closed as a through route in 1960, the colliery became the only source of traffic on the remaining branch from Colwick and Netherfield. No 56058 is about to depart from the colliery sidings with the 7F80 'mgr' train to Ratcliffe on 29 October 1986.

The colliery closed in 1991, but the branch re-opened briefly in 1998/99 to allow the removal of coal from the spoil heaps by rail. The run-round loop that was provided for the latter traffic is pictured on 2 July 2005. Plans to re-open the Gedling branch for passenger traffic as part of the Greater Nottingham Area Railway Development System have come to nothing. *Both PDS*

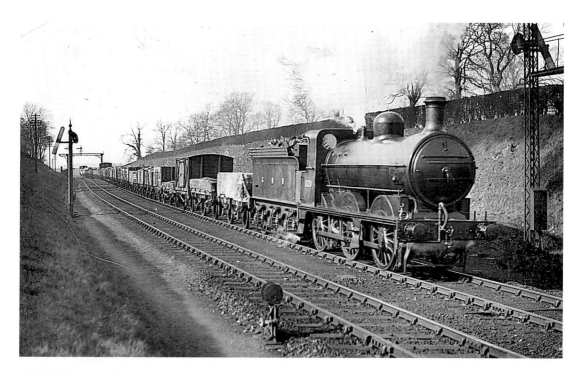

RADCLIFFE: Great Northern Railway Class 'J3' 0-6-0 No 1120 approaches Radcliffe-on-Trent with an eastbound mixed goods train in 1923. This locomotive class was formed in 1912 by rebuilding some of the 'J4s', originally introduced in 1896. A few 'J3s' survived into BR stock, but all were withdrawn by the early 1950s.

The location today is recognisable from the curve of the track, but a housing estate is now well established on the north side of the line and the neatly tended cutting side and boundary hedge seen in the 'past' photograph have given way to an informal nature reserve. Unit No 170630 forms the 0747 Liverpool Lime Street to Norwich service on 31 August 2005. *John Ward collection/PDS*

RADCLIFFE: The up (eastbound) platform at Radcliffe-on-Trent is pictured from a passing train on 8 July 1948, just six months after nationalisation. In the distance is a GNR junction somersault signal.

Radcliffe lost its station staff when BR introduced 'paytrain' operation to the Nottingham-Grantham line in 1968. At least that meant that the station was less vulnerable to closure; at the time of writing it is reasonably well used and enjoys direct services to Skegness, Norwich, Crewe and Liverpool. On 31 August 2005 unit No 170634 approaches the station with 0757 service from Norwich to Liverpool Lime Street. *H. C. Casserley/PDS*

ASLOCKTON: Former LNER Class 'L1' 2-6-4T No 67800 pulls away from Aslockton station with the 1.20pm train from Derby Friargate to Grantham on 7 November 1962. This train will have been routed via Basford North and Nottingham Victoria, using a short stretch of the ex-GCR main line before regaining former GNR metals at Weekday Cross Junction.

The public footpath from which the 'past' photograph was taken still exists today and has not yet been separated from the railway by high-security fencing. Unit No 170115 heads east with the 0952 Liverpool Lime Street to Norwich service on 7 June 2005. *David Holmes/PDS*

ELTON & ORSTON: With the winter sun casting long shadows in the shallow cutting, Class 'L1' 2-6-4T No 67798 calls at Elton & Orston with the 1.36pm Grantham to Nottingham Victoria train on 19 December 1962. Already the station platforms look unkempt, but the wooden shelter on the up platform appears to be still in use.

The train service at Elton & Orston at the time of writing comprises just two eastbound and two westbound departures each weekday, with the westbound departures well separated at 0735 and 2204! Unit No 170634 speeds towards Nottingham as the 0957 service from Norwich to Liverpool Lime Street on 7 June 2005. *David Holmes/PDS*

LOWFIELD: Although it was never an important passenger route and saw its last scheduled passenger train in 1953, the line from Bottesford West Junction to Newark South Junction remained open for freight until 1987, in later years being used mainly by oil trains between Immingham and the Total oil terminal at Colwick (Rectory Junction). No 56085 pauses for token exchange at Lowfield box, just south of Newark, with 7E38, the 0954 Rectory Junction to Immingham empty tank train, on 31 July 1984.

BR was able to close the Bottesford to Newark line with relatively little adverse impact; the oil trains were diverted via Nottingham in the outward direction and via Grantham on the return journey. The former freight line has been converted into a pleasant and useful cycle track and footpath, as seen on 25 July 2005. *Both PDS*

LOWDHAM: The Midland Railway signal box dating back to 1896 overlooks the level crossing as Fowler Class 4 2-6-4T passes through with a parcels and empty coaching stock train from Nottingham to Lincoln on 22 August 1959.

Nearly 46 years later, on 25 July 2005, the box is still in use and looking somewhat smarter than in the earlier view, being now a Grade 2-listed structure. On the station platform a second generation of electric lighting has been installed and more signs have appeared to guide passengers to the correct exit. Unit No 158780 forms the 1532 service from Leicester to Grimsby Town. *Milepost 92½ (H. B. Priestley)/PDS*

LOWDHAM still had its wheel-operated level crossing gates and co-acting semaphore signals when this photograph was taken on 30 July 1984. A Swindon Class 120 unit comprising cars M53670, M59524 and M53744 forms the 1520 service from Crewe to Lincoln St Marks.

Partial resignalling took place shortly after the date of the 'past' photograph and the level crossing now has full lifting barriers. A three-car train comprising units Nos 156410 and 153376 makes its call as the 1535 service from Lincoln Central to Leicester on 25 July 2005. The semaphores at the east end of the station survive, as does the engineers' siding on the down side. *Both PDS*

BLEASBY: The Nottingham to Lincoln line carried heavy mineral traffic as well as a well-used passenger service. Class 4F 0-6-0 No 44215 heads towards Nottingham with a train of unfitted coal wagons on 11 May 1957. Bleasby was the only station between Nottingham and Newark never to have had a signal box; the crossing-keeper used a small hut with an external frame.

The up platform has been relocated on the west side of the crossing to reduce delays to road traffic when a Nottingham-bound train calls at the station. The brick-built booking office has gone, but the station house on the extreme right survives, albeit in rather poor condition. The 'present' photograph is dated 25 July 2005. *Milepost 92½ (H. B. Priestley)/PDS*

ROLLESTON station was formerly the junction for Southwell, but it was already reduced to a two-platform unstaffed halt when this scene was recorded on 27 May 1974. The crossing-keeper on the down platform watches a three-car Class 120 unit arriving as the 1835 Lincoln St Marks to Derby service. The neatly tended vegetable garden adds a homely touch.

Rolleston still has its level crossing with manually worked gates, but the keeper's hut has been relocated next to the crossing, behind the photographer. The road is a minor one and the gates are normally kept open for the railway; however, traffic builds up quickly when there is racing at Southwell. No 66200 rolls through the station with 6M88, the 1223 Immingham to Ketton coal train, on 25 July 2005. *Michael Mensing/PDS*

ROLLESTON: Standing in the branch platform at Rolleston Junction on 2 April 1959 is Class 'A5' 4-6-2T No 69803 with the 3.45pm departure to Southwell. The passenger service over the 2½-mile branch was to be withdrawn as an economy measure just two months later. In the background is Rolleston Junction signal box, a classic Midland Railway structure dating back to the 1870s.

The branch tracks remained in use for coal traffic from Mansfield until the mid-1960s. Since then the site of the branch platforms has become overgrown, although just behind the photographer part of the trackbed has been converted into a private road. An oil train from Immingham to Kingsbury is partly obscured by undergrowth as it passes through the surviving station behind a Freightliner Class 66 on 25 July 2005. *David Holmes/PDS*

SOUTHWELL: The Midland Railway bypassed the small cathedral city of Southwell when it opened its Nottingham to Lincoln line in 1846, and it had to make do with a branch line from Rolleston, which used horse traction in its early years, a permanent steam-hauled service not being introduced until 1860. Despite its uncertain beginnings, the Midland provided Southwell station with a fine house beside the level crossing, pictured here from the west on 9 June 1956.

Although now surrounded by modern development, the station house is still lived in and retains its original architectural detail, as seen on 25 July 2005. It was on the market at that time for £310,000. *H. C. Casserley/PDS*

SOUTHWELL became a through station in 1870 with the opening of the 12½-mile line from Mansfield. The through line became an important outlet for traffic from the new collieries east of Mansfield, and in 1929 the LMS invested in two line improvements – the doubling of the existing line from Southwell to Rolleston Junction and a new south-facing curve to Fiskerton. On 2 April 1959 Stanier 8F 2-8-0 No 48763 heads east through Southwell with a train of mainly wooden-bodied mineral wagons.

The station site was sold for redevelopment, but a car park on the west side of the level crossing marks the start of the attractive Southwell Trail, extending to Farnsfield and Bilsthorpe. The 'present' view is dated 25 July 2005.
David Holmes/PDS

KIRKLINGTON: The Mansfield to Southwell line failed to attract adequate passenger numbers and timetabled trains were withdrawn as early as 1929. However, the line continued to see excursion traffic and race specials. The forlorn intermediate station of Kirklington is pictured on 12 April 1952, with Class 4F 0-6-0 No 44425 heading an excursion towards Southwell.

The line closed to all traffic in 1965, with coal from the Mansfield area to Lincolnshire being diverted over the former GCR line via Clipstone and Tuxford. The station house at Kirklington has, however, stood the test of time and is now a handsome private residence, well hidden by trees from the glances of walkers on the Southwell Trail, as seen on 29 April 2006. *Milepost 92½ (H. B. Priestley)/PDS*

NEWARK CASTLE: The Midland was the first railway company to reach Newark, beating the Great Northern by two years. Its two-platform through station was accompanied by extensive goods sidings and a warehouse at the Lincoln end. About three-quarters of a mile beyond the station the Great Northern crossed the Midland on the level – one of three such crossings on the East Coast route, of which only Newark survives today. The Midland station is pictured facing Lincoln in 1906.

Just under a century later, on 31 August 2005, the similarities are more striking than the differences. The canopies have gone but most of the buildings are still there, including the warehouse now partly hidden by trees, and the platforms retain their differing lengths. A colour light signal now protects the crossing, but the signalling is still controlled from the Midland Railway box just out of sight to the right of the picture. *R. M. Casserley collection/PDS*

COLLINGHAM is the first station beyond Newark on the former Midland line to Lincoln. Passing what seems to be a remarkably large house for a small station, Class 4F 0-6-0 No 43917 heads a mixed goods train towards Lincoln on 30 July 1959.

Collingham became an unstaffed halt in 1969, together with other intermediate stations on the Nottingham-Lincoln line. Its platforms have been raised to modern safety standards and the modest station furniture has been renewed. At the time of writing it is served by ten trains in each direction on weekdays; on 25 July 2005 single-car No 153379 recedes towards Newark forming the 1335 service from Lincoln Central to Leicester. *Milepost 92½ (H. B. Priestley)/PDS*

NEWARK NORTH GATE: The Class 55 'Deltics' enjoyed only a short reign on top-rank East Coast Main Line expresses from their introduction in 1961 to their replacement by High Speed Train (later InterCity 125) sets in 1978. After that they were relegated to semi-fast duties, until final withdrawals took place in January 1981. No 55021 *Argyll and Sutherland Highlander* departs from Newark with the 1550 York to London King's Cross semi-fast service on 30 May 1980, while station pilot No 08137 rests between duties.

A similar view today can be taken from the cycle track that follows the former railway route towards Bottesford West Junction. An InterCity 225 formation heads south forming the 1405 Leeds to Finsbury Park service on 29 April 2006 – stopping short of its usual King's Cross destination because of engineering work. The shift to fixed-formation passenger trains and the loss of parcels and freight traffic at Newark have long since made the station pilot redundant. *Both PDS*

Newark,
Great Northern Railway Station.

NEWARK NORTH GATE: This fascinating portrait shows the Great Northern station in Newark with its full complement of waiting rooms, refreshment rooms, 'ladies' and 'gents', and other essential facilities for the long-distance traveller of the late 19th century. Signs and posters abound, some of them advertising well-known and enduring brands such as Bovril and – partly hidden behind the station staff on the down platform – Pears Soap.

Much of the original ironwork survives on the down platform, as does the Potts clock – visible just to the left of the train. However, the up-side buildings and footbridge have been replaced and the up platform itself looks new. An InterCity 125 unit departs forming the 1730 London King's Cross to Skipton train on 23 July 2005, a train that has to be diesel-operated because of electric power supply limitations between Leeds and Skipton. *Lens of Sutton/PDS*

CROW PARK: The East Coast Main Line crosses a mainly flat landscape on the eastern fringe of Nottinghamshire, with numerous level crossings. At Crow Park, roughly halfway between Newark and Retford, an overbridge had already superseded the level crossing for the Great North Road by the late 1940s, although the crossing remained in use for local traffic. Class 'A1' 4-6-2 No 60116 *Hal o' the Wynd* heads south with the 9.04am Sunderland to London King's Cross express on 30 June 1962.

The 'A1s' have been replaced by three successive generations of motive power – Class 55 'Deltics', diesel InterCity 125s and electric InterCity 225s. An InterCity 225 set rushes north on 23 July 2005 forming the 1630 service from London King's Cross to Leeds. The former crossing box has gone, but the crossing-keeper's house beside it survives. *David Holmes/PDS*

TUXFORD was once an important railway location with exchange sidings between the GNR East Coast Main Line and the GCR Chesterfield to Lincoln line. Class 'A2' 4-6-2 No 60502 *Earl Marischal* passes the GNR signal box with the down 'Queen of Scots' Pullman on 20 August 1960. The former GCR line ran across the bridge in the distance and was connected to GNR metals via the double-track curve on the right. Until 1950 there was also a two-level interchange station at the intersection, named Dukeries Junction.

Today mature trees obscure the abandoned formation of the exchange sidings and connecting curve. A Class 91-hauled InterCity 225 train heads north on 23 July 2005. *David Holmes/PDS*

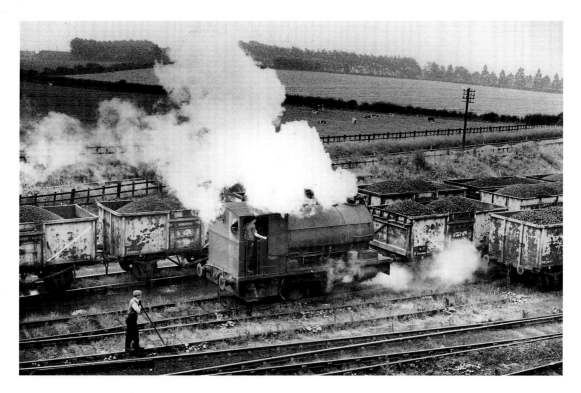

North Nottinghamshire

STEETLEY Colliery was sunk in 1873, just before the opening of the railway from Mansfield to Worksop. With the main line running across the picture between the two wooden fences, Peckett 0-4-0ST No 2109 shunts 16-ton mineral wagons in the colliery sidings on 25 August 1967.

The last coal from Steetley was wound in 1983 and much of the site is now a vast post-industrial wasteland. The name Steetley lives on, not because of the colliery but because of the major industrial organisation that developed out of a modest quarrying operation at this location in 1885. The 'present' photograph is dated 23 July 2005. *Roger Siviter/PDS*

WHITWELL: The line from Mansfield to Worksop is never far from the Nottinghamshire/Derbyshire boundary and crosses it several times; Whitwell lies just within Derbyshire. Its colliery was sunk in 1890, 15 years after the opening of the railway, and was still thriving in the early 1980s, with production levels exceeding 500,000 tonnes a year. Nos 20008 and 20026 leave the colliery sidings on 15 April 1983 with the 6T61 trip working to Worksop, conveying HTV hoppers with domestic coal for Grimsby.

Whitwell pit never recovered from the 1984 miners' strike and closed in 1986. The adjacent quarry produced some rail traffic in the early 1990s, but after that the remaining sidings at Whitwell fell into disuse. A new passenger station opened in 1998 for the 'Robin Hood Line' extension to Worksop, and unit No 156413 departs as the 1340 service from Worksop to Nottingham on 23 July 2005. *Both PDS*

117

SHIREOAKS: The mining town of Shireoaks lay on the GCR's Sheffield to Retford line, but the station was also used by Midland Railway trains from the Mansfield line and, from 1910, by trains on the South Yorkshire Joint Line to Doncaster. With at least two photographers standing on the adjacent running line – imagine trying that today! – Class 'B1' 4-6-0 No 61166 awaits departure with the RCTS 'South Yorkshire Railtour' on 11 May 1952. The train had just run round in the station and was on the last leg of its journey back to Sheffield after visiting two branches of the Hull & Barnsley Railway.

The station became an unstaffed halt in 1969, but the building on the eastbound platform survives today, although no longer in railway use. Freightliner Heavy Haul No 66531 heads west with coal empties on 23 July 2005. *John Edgington/PDS*

SHIREOAKS: The area around Worksop and Shireoaks was a long-lived pocket of manual signalling. Passing Shireoaks East Junction box on 24 July 1984 is a Class 114 unit comprising cars E54016 and E53032 forming the 1612 Retford to Sheffield service. Two further boxes can be seen in the distance: Worksop Sidings and Worksop Station West.

The line was resignalled in 1997/98 and the three boxes visible in the 'past' photograph were abolished. This was the scene on 23 July 2005, with a trio of EWS Class 66 locomotives waiting in Worksop yard for their next duty. Despite the demise of most local collieries, Worksop is still a key location for EWS coal traffic. *Both PDS*

WORKSOP: Class 'WD' 'Austerity' 2-8-0 No 90129 heads west through Worksop with a lengthy rake of empty mineral wagons on 18 April 1964. The 'WDs' were used on heavy freight work and were spread across all BR regions except the Southern.

Most of the steam-age features of the 'past' photograph have disappeared, including the footbridge, which must have been relatively new in 1964. But Worksop East signal box, a Manchester Sheffield & Lincolnshire Railway structure dating back to around 1880, still stands, albeit no longer controlling any semaphores. No 66509 heads west with empty HHA hoppers from either Cottam or West Burton power station on 22 July 2005. *Ray Ruffell, Silver Link Publishing collection/PDS*

RETFORD: The GCR line from Sheffield crossed the GNR East Coast Main Line on the level at Retford. Originally there were no platforms on the GCR line; any GCR trains serving Retford had to use two connecting curves to call at the GNR platforms. Class 'O4' 2-8-0 No 63688 heads an eastbound freight on the ex-GCR route on 24 October 1964.

BR abolished the flat crossing in 1965 by lowering the ex-GCR line and building a bridge beneath the East Coast Main Line. At the same time new platforms were provided on the ex-GCR route. The curve on the west side of Retford was retained to allow movements between the ECML and Sheffield, but the shorter curve on the east side of the station was removed. The 'present' scene is dated 23 July 2005. *Paul Forbes/PDS*

RETFORD boasted two small engine sheds, one on the GNR line on the down side of Retford station and the other on the GCR line just beside Thrumpton crossing, a quarter of a mile east of the station. Class 'O4/3' 2-8-0 No 63702 is pictured under the shear-legs at the GCR shed on 24 October 1964. After nationalisation the two Retford sheds carried the same code, 36E.

The former GCR shed closed in January 1965, while the ex-GNR facility lasted five months longer. The GCR site was undergoing redevelopment on 23 July 2005. *Paul Forbes/PDS*

RETFORD: Although dogged by failure and withdrawn prematurely after just a few years' service, the prototype 'Deltic' was a bold venture by English Electric to launch a new generation of motive power on Britain's railways and paved the way for the building of 22 production series locomotives. Its stylish livery and distinctive single headlamp housing mounted on the front nose – intended for use in Canada – are seen to good effect in this view of the down 'White Rose' arriving at Retford on 25 September 1959. On the far left of the picture is the curved platform that was used by trains on the ex-GCR line to Gainsborough.

Retford station was remodelled in 1976 to allow higher speeds on the fast lines. The down platform is now situated between the slow and fast lines but serves the slow line only. Hull Trains unit No 222104 arrives with the 1612 London King's Cross to Hull service on 31 August 2005. *Ron Robinson/PDS*

RETFORD: Class 'A3' 4-6-2 No 60110 *Robert the Devil* stands at Retford with an up semi-fast train composed of BR Standard Mark I stock, on 25 September 1959. The shedplate 34A shows that the locomotive was allocated to King's Cross. The sign advertising Earle's Cement refers to the works in the Hope Valley that is now owned by Lafarge, the original owner's name living on in the exchange sidings by the main line. The poster to the left of the fire buckets declares 'Cesspools Emptied' and illustrates a state-of-the-art lorry that would presumably have removed the effluent.

While the original down platform was swept away by the 1970s remodelling, the up platform and the main station buildings have changed relatively little. On 31 August 2005 a displaced Eurostar train comprising sets 3310 and 3309 forms the 1705 service from Leeds to London King's Cross. Train operator GNER hired three Eurostar trains from 2000 until December 2005 to provide increased capacity on the London-Leeds route. *Ron Robinson/PDS*

MISTERTON: The Doncaster to Gainsborough line passes through the north-east corner of Nottinghamshire. Originally owned jointly by the GNR and GER, the line was a useful route for freight avoiding the busy East Coast Main Line. Class 'O2' 2-8-0 No 63925 passes Misterton with a northbound mixed freight on 28 April 1962.

Misterton closed to passengers in 1961 and to goods in 1969, but the goods shed still stands today, as pictured on 23 July 2005. The line supports a sparse passenger service and some through freight traffic, although there is plenty of capacity for more. *David Holmes/PDS*

FIRBECK: The 17½-mile South Yorkshire Joint Line from Kirk Sandall Junction, near Doncaster, to Dinnington Junction, near Shireoaks, was a late addition to the railway network, opening to goods in 1909 and to passengers in 1910. The passenger service lasted only until 1929, but since then the line has proved to be a useful through route for coal and other freight traffic as well as serving local collieries such as Maltby and Harworth. Nos 20015 and 20154 take the Harworth branch at Firbeck West Junction with 6T68, the 'mgr' empties from West Burton, on 13 April 1983.

The semaphore signals have gone, but the South Yorkshire Joint Line is still in daily use. The 'present' photograph is dated 22 July 2005. *Both PDS*

HARWORTH Colliery was established between 1919 and 1924, and a branch was laid from the South Yorkshire Joint Line to serve it. Leaving the exchange sidings on 13 April 1983 are Nos 20208 and 20133 with the 6T64 trip working to Worksop, conveying domestic coal for Grimsby in MCV mineral wagons. The sidings also contain two types of air-braked stock: HAA 'merry-go-round' hoppers and HBA manual-discharge hoppers. The single line on the right served Harworth Glass Bulbs, which at that time forwarded traffic in ferry vans.

The exchange sidings were abandoned as the railway concentrated on running whole trainloads of coal. The simplified track layout on the approach to the pit is pictured on 22 July 2005. Harworth subsequently wound its last coal in August 2006, despite significant investment in opening up new reserves during its final months. *Both PDS*

INDEX OF LOCATIONS